COLLABORATIVE PRECARITY BODYHACKING
WORK-BOOK AND RESOURCE GUIDE

for 'resistance fantasies'
@ the exponential festival

january 2019, this edition 2021

cory tamler, elæ moss & stormy budwig,
facilitators

THE
"COLLABORATIVE PRECARITY BODYHACKING
WORK-BOOK AND RESOURCE GUIDE"
c. 2018-2019, this edition c. 2021
ISBN# 978-1-946031-96-9
Library of Congress CIP # 2021947353

was
DEVELOPED BY
cory tamler, elæ moss
& stormy budwig, facilitators

EDITED AND DESIGNED BY
ELÆ MOSS

and

is published under a
CREATIVE COMMONS
CC BY-NC-ND 4.0 license
https://creativecommons.org/licenses/by-nc-nd/4.0/
by
THE OPERATING SYSTEM / THE TROUBLE WITH BARTLEBY
BROOKLYN/LENAPEHOKING AND WORLDWIDE
WWW.THEOPERATINGSYSTEM.ORG

WITH THANKS TO:

THE EXPONENTIAL FESTIVAL
THERESA BUCHHEISTER
and
in memory of ANGSTROM (a very good cat)

DEAR READER / USER / HUMAN:

We are so glad that this work-book has made it into your hands. In the pages that follow you will find prompts and exercises, an experimental collaborative score, notes and resources, as well as ample room for you to add your own additions, work, or projects. These materials not only bridge genres -- encompassing writing, movement, somatic experiencing, performance / theater, mindfulness, and more -- but also invite and encourage you to tear down these illusory distinctions, as well as any limitations you've been conditioned to understand define who is supposed to participate in these disciplines, and in what way. This work seeks to trouble our social, cultural, public and private patterning, and so too turns that reverse engineering on itself: how can, how must, we reframe our relationship to all the tools and media at our disposal, in the service of learning how to live with each other, and our selves, in these bodies, in these times and places (and in whatever future is to come?)

This document was originally produced in tandem with the collaborative precarity bodyhacking workshop we developed as part of 'resistance fantasies' for the Exponential Theatre Festival in 2019, but is envisioned as a emergent document with infinitely malleable potential: for those who have taken this workshop, it can be used in session, and then you can continue using this work-book as a tool to strengthen and continue exploring and building on the work we've done together. For those who are coming to it fresh, this book offers an auto-didactic entrance into self-exploration of body, mind, language, communication, perception, and more. For either of these groups, the tools and resources collected here can be used as an open source jumping off point for your own community explorations: roundtables, reading groups, writing groups, workshops, for use in your classroom or community organization, or via your own iteration(s)f of the score. Or any number of ways we can't begin to imagine.

We are here as askers of questions, inviting you in with us to better know ourselves, together.

Thank you for trusting us with this part of your journey.

Cory, Elæ, and stormy

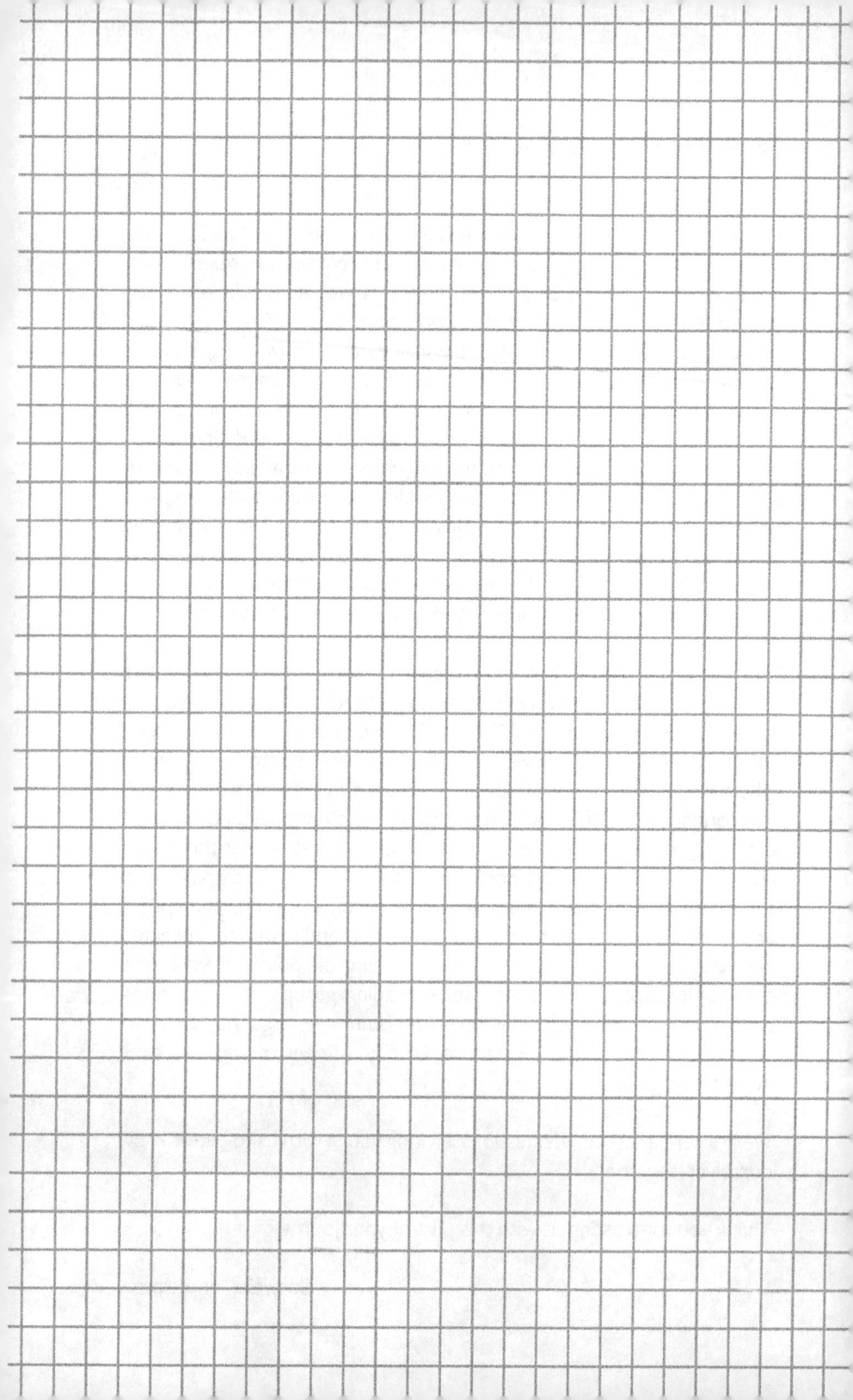

TABLE OF CONTENTS:

DEFINITIONS & KEY TERMS

HACKING (SELF vs. BODY vs. BIO): a play on the contemporary understanding of 'hack' as an act of going in the back end of a computer or computer system, applied to becoming agentive in your own reprogramming and human system operation. "SELFHACKING" could be the umbrella term for any personally oriented reprogramming work, utilizing language, mindfulness, breathing, somatics, etc. Here we use "BODYHACKING" to describe specifically working with awareness of the body and its sensory, perceptual, proprioceptic condition in order to make changes in our system / life. "BIOHACKING" is a more radical version of SELF/BODY-HACKING, involving actual manipulation of human systems via chemical, biological, surgical, or other means.

MINDFULNESS - associated primarily with meditative practices, now widely applied in secular settings, we use and refer to "MINDFULNESS" techniques and exercises to shift and direct our focus, often integrating this practice with BREATHWORK, which in turn influences the PARASYMPATHETIC NERVOUS SYSTEM and the BRAIN. Now widely used in therapeutic settings, in COGNITIVE BEHAVIOR THERAPY and other healing systems. Perhaps our earliest human "self-and-body hacking" practice.

PRECARITY - PRECARITY is 'non-self-determined insecurity' across work and life (Raunig, 2004), with insecure access to means to survive or flourish (Precarias, 2004). As a term, it was first picked up by European social and labor movements in the 1970s to advocate for better work/life conditions for those in contingent, flexible, or irregular employment. It operates by rendering people's lives 'contingent on capital' (Mitropoulos, 2005). Precarity leads to 'yo-yo hours and days' which interfere with human contact (Tarì and Vanni, 2005) and eliminate the sense of a distinct future, due to time-space compression (Neilson and Rossiter, n.d.) or 'present shock' (Rushkoff, 2013). It corrodes one's ability to distinguish life from work (Fantone, 2006). The affective effects of this situation contribute to anxiety. People are constantly over-stimulated by information and sensory input which over-engages attention (2009:

97, 115), leading to a 'constant attentive stress' (2009: 42) (Institute for Precarious Consciousness, 2014: 277).

Butler, and others, use "precarity" to talk about not just the condition of precarious work but the existential and social condition of a life that feels risky, uncertain, and unstable, which is unequally distributed in society across different kinds of bodies based on gender, class, ethnicity, citizenship, etc. [definition from "Why does everyone I know feel so anxious?" - Eliot Feenstra, June 2018]

SEDIMENTATION - in natural processes, SEDIMENTATION is defined as "the tendency for particles in suspension to settle and come to rest." Here we apply this term to our relationship to new ideas / concepts / practices as they enter, form, suspend, and eventually settle in our systems.

SCORE - for our purposes, understood as an experimental set of instructions via which we reframe our ordinary, conditioned behaviors, allowing us to experience a diversion from programmed perceptions / interactions / sensations. (See "more scores and instructions, p 57)

SOMATICS - commonly framed as a field within bodywork and movement studies which emphasizes physical perception and experience, understood more broadly the integration of SOMATICS into creative practice and/or lived behavior includes any techniques by which we might attend more intentionally to the SOMA, or "the body as perceived from within." (for more, and exercises, see p. 47)

HOW TO USE THIS WORK-BOOK

The workshop structure is this book's organizing principle. Loosely, the structure is as follows: we begin with introductions, protocols to guide our work together, definitions, and individual writing prompts to focus our thoughts. We then start to work on our bodies, exploring ways of listening, observing, and interacting that begin to uncover physical and emotional programming. Building on these exercises, we share a score (or series of instructions/guidelines) intended to guide the group in trying out the ideas and ways of moving we've collectively developed.

In this work-book, you will first find the workshop outline, prompts and space for note-taking as used in our workshop, and a basic outline of our culminating score. These all follow the structure of the workshop. They are followed by a "Resources" section intended for anyone interested in leading a workshop. In "Resources," there are descriptions in detail of the exercises we used, supplementary exercises/explanations/readings, and a more detailed version of our culminating score alongside sample scores. You will also find an alphabetical annotated bibliography that draws together precarity-relevant writing in the fields of somatics, theatre and performance studies, performance and bodywork practices, queer and feminist theory, mindfulness, emergent strategy and network theories, social choreography, applied theatre, and more. Prompts and exercises will cross-reference the bibliography, so you can follow our sources and explore for yourself.

We invite you to make use of the materials here as a resource for study—or for creating a workshop of your own. Be in dialogue with us about what you make. Expanding and strengthening the networks we want is at the core of this work.

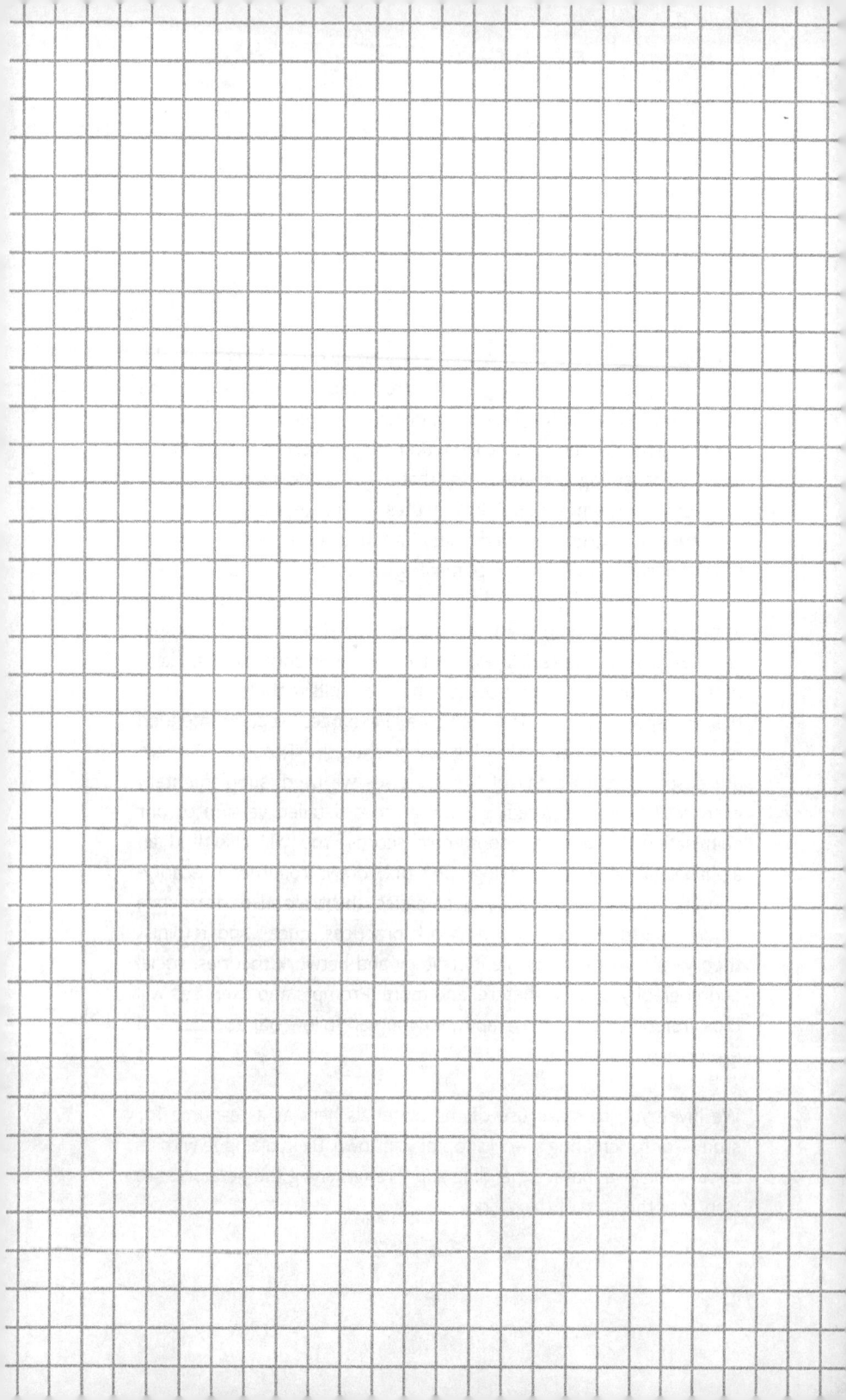

SAMPLE SCHEDULES / EXERCISES
FOR 1 & 2 DAY WORKSHOP SESSIONS

In our sessions at the Exponential Theater festival, we held two different workshops sessions, for 2 days of 4 hours each and a single day for 5 hours. What this section contains is a literal "work-book," following the structure of these sessions, both for use by participants as well as for others who may want to either investigate these exercises on their own and/or in community. Room has been left for note-taking as one works through this section.

Immediately following this section are frameworks for each session type, additional notes on the prompts and processes used, as well as alternatives you may want to try or use in your own facilitation.

2 DAY WORKSHOP [4 HRS / DAY]

Day 1

Intro: Basic concepts and Intentions
Begin with Breathing (4/7)
Precarity Interview & Short Prompts for in-class writing
Writing / Mindfulness / Beginning Somatic Orientation prompts
Somatics Based Movement Warm-Up
Repetitions and Observations Technique Exercise
Writing Prompts
Authentic Movement

Day 2

Review concepts and Intentions, feedback on day 1
Begin with Breathing (4/7)
Writing Prompt: Sedimentation
Somatics Based Movement Warm-Up
SCORE

----

1 DAY WORKSHOP [5 HOURS]

Breathwork
Prompts / Somatic Mindfulness
Somatic Movement
Mindfulness / Breathwork / Guided Writing
Performance Exercises / Score
Sedimentation / Documentation

DAY 1

OPENING PROMPT

How are you feeling / sensing today?

What sensations arise as you consider
what you perceive as your risks / limitations?

What would you invite in / allow for / prioritize in your life
if you felt there was no risk or loss possible as a result?
What would you change in terms of your time, energy, body,
environment, the people in your life, the choices you make, etc.?

What would it feel like to be this person in this possible space?

PRECARITY / INTERPERSONAL INFRASTRUCTURES
SELF-ASSESSMENT

These questions are intended to help you sketch out the systemic conditions of your situation. You may wish to answer these one at a time, or review them all, taken as a thematic prompt, and answer in paragraph form.

Do you feel like you have adequate resources?

What resources, structures, or relationships do you have that function well for you, if any?

Are these resources emotional, interpersonal, financial, familial, a mix of these?

What resources, structures, or relationships aren't working for you?

Do you feel precarious in your financial, physical health / safety, professional life or in other areas? How, and why? For how long have you felt precarious? Do you feel trapped in any way? In relationships, jobs, housing, debt, etc? Is this related to a feeling of precarity or resource/systemic insecurity?

Do you feel like you are seen / read / perceived accurately vis-a-vis your relationship to resources / security? How / how not, when / when not. Are you able to represent yourself honestly? What keeps you performing and/or hiding aspects of your relationship to resources and systems? Does this affect you?

What choices have you made in your life as a result of feelings of precarity, fear, or lack of adequate resources?

In what ways do you feel like your feelings of precarity or fear around resources are personal vs. systemic?

Do you feel (or have you been made to feel) like the precarity of your situation is somehow your fault?

What do you feel you would have done differently in your life if you weren't fearful about resources? (In terms of relationships, education, career/work and job choices, housing, health and wellness, family, etc)

What would you do differently, now, if all concerns about resources and systemic lack of support were erased? (In terms of relationships, education, career/work and job choices, housing, health and wellness, family, etc)

Do you feel like you are ever able to make choices without fear of systemic danger? When and how have you felt like this the most or least? How does it affect you now?

Do you feel adequately supported in your lifework, passions or creative practice? Why or why not?

Has your creative practice (or other central identity) been a source of discord, alienation, or othering in your life?

What are your most present challenges in feeling adequately connected and supported? (location, finances, health, schedule, etc)

What resources do you rely on to help you address these challenges?

In what ways do things go unaddressed, and why?

Do you feel like you are a member of any or multiple "communities"? Which, and for how long? What does the nature of your engagement constitute in terms of activity, connection, resources, etc.?

Do you feel like the communities you'd like to be a part of are fully accessible to you? Why/how or why not/how not?

If you are a member of groups or communities, how are these communities supportive, or how not?

What aspects of your community experience feel intentional, desired, or aligned with your goals / values? (or don't)

How does social media or virtual community play into your feelings of connection (or alienation)? Why and how?

Do you find that you actively use social media as a stopgap or replacement for in person connection?

Do you find that you feel trapped by social media, but feel you can't leave it for a variety of reasons?

In what ways is your relationship to social media use / reliance connected to feelings of lack in other areas?

Have you spent much time or other resources on visioning, planning, or actively building an organization, cooperative, community, or business, either on your own or with a partner or team?

How has this affected your ability to maintain, access, or establish resources for yourself, either positively or negatively? How has this changed your relationship to others, communities, or your practice?

Have you spent much time or other resources proactively visioning or planning what sort of communities, kinship structures, networks, relationships, infrastructures, or resources you would like to see for yourself, your discipline, your personal practice, your neighborhood, or beyond?

Have you felt like you had the choice or ability to actively question the relationships or systems you have relied on?

Alternately, were you forced to question or build relationships or systems of your own? Why/how? Did this help or hinder your feelings of agency in other parts of your life? What if anything was abandoned or sacrificed as a result?

What sorts of structures would you have / build / rely on if it was possible and you felt resources were available?

Do you think it might be possible to re-examine the way we use and distribute resources (time, money, labor) in order to build these systems?

Would you be willing to participate, consistently, in this sort of building? If your immediate reaction is that it is impossible, do you think that this is because of fear or reliance on old systems? Are you scared to fail at building and risk the loss of old structures and relationships, even if they aren't working?

Do you feel like you have a responsibility to create change or be an engaged citizen? Do you feel like everyone has the privilege to do so? Why or why not? If you don't feel you have this privilege, how do you feel that you can be supported or be part of intentional change along these areas of investigation?

ADDITIONAL DEMOGRAPHIC INFORMATION:

HOUSING: (ie: roommates, live alone, partnered, rent, own, live with parents, intentional community)

LABOR / EMPLOYMENT:

FINANCIALS : (family support, debt, dependents, medical or other invisible expenses, etc)

SCHOOLING / DEGREES:

CREATIVE PRACTICE:

RACE / ETHNICITY:

GENDER / PRONOUN:

SEXUAL ORIENTATION:

DISABILITY or CHRONIC ILLNESS?

CARETAKER or PARENT?

FURTHER NOTES ON PRECARITY

FURTHER NOTES ON PRECARITY

SOMATICS BASED MOVEMENT* WARM-UP

NOTES & OBSERVATIONS

*SEE RESOURCES FOR MORE EXERCISES & BACKGROUND INFO

REPETITIONS AND OBSERVATIONS EXERCISE*

Your task is to notice as many true things as possible about your partner and to write them down. Do not stop writing. Your partner will not read what you write, nor will anyone else. Among your true things, include:

the objective (green eyes, striped shirt)
the subjective (they're nervous, they're open, they're uncertain)
the speculative (they're a journalist, they have a big family, they're conservative, they grew up in a city)

Notes after Repetitions

Notes after Extended Eye Contact

FURTHER NOTES & OBSERVATIONS

FURTHER NOTES & OBSERVATIONS

FURTHER NOTES & OBSERVATIONS

PROMPT / CHECK IN:

How are you feeling / sensing right now?

Do you notice any changes in your body from how you felt
when we first checked in at the beginning of this session?
What sort of changes? Can you describe any differences
in your perception of energy and/or awareness in relationship
to your body / your surroundings / others?

PROMPT:

Reflect on some tools this workshop has provided so far, especially in terms of living with, inside of, and from your body. What strategies have you already developed to move through the world? Had you recognized them as strategies? How will you pass these Somatic tools / strategies on to your community(ies)? Who do you know who might need this work?

PROMPT:

Do you feel like you are seen / read / perceived accurately
vis-a-vis your relationship to resources / security?
How / how not, when / when not?
Are you able to represent yourself honestly?
What keeps you performing and/or hiding aspects of your
relationship to resources and systems? Does this affect you?
How do you want to be seen and why do you want to be seen this way?

AUTHENTIC MOVEMENT* EXERCISE

NOTES & OBSERVATIONS

*SEE RESOURCES FOR MORE EXERCISES & BACKGROUND INFO

REFLECTIONS / NOTES ON DAY 1

DAY 2

CHECK IN / SEDIMENTATION

How are you feeling/sensing?
Is it different from how you entered or left yesterday? How?

What did you carry with you into your experiences both public and
private since leaving this space yesterday?
What, if anything, do you want to bring into today's session
in terms of your mind / body / energy based on what you
experienced yesterday or in the interim?

Highlight three things from yesterday's session that you want to bring into the room / your mind / body today, and consider the terms of bringing this forward / to awareness.

SOMATICS BASED MOVEMENT* WARM-UP

NOTES & OBSERVATIONS

*SEE RESOURCES FOR MORE EXERCISES & BACKGROUND INFO

*SCORE PARAMETERS / INSTRUCTIONS AS FOLLOWED FOR THIS WORKSHOP, p. 55; MORE SCORES & BACKGROUND INFO, p.57 AND IN RESOURCE SECTION

"INTER/FACINGS" : A SCORE WE MADE and USED*

being / sensing / interacting / moving / mapping
as a troubling of
perception, communication, collaboration & building

*In this score we will bring both independent and collective
wants / vocabularies / perceptions, and objectives into play.
Before we begin we will each map our own contributions, as
well as collectively determine shared definitions / signals.*

*gestures / movements / sounds / post-its and other assignations
are all potential materials for this taxonomy*

PROMPTS / EMERGENT MAPPING:

FIRST, IDENTIFY:

1 thing you personally want to do (private want)
1 thing you want other individuals to do (interpersonal want)
1 thing you want other people to do as a group (public want)

BRAINSTORM:
TERMS / VOCABULARY / SPATIAL DEFINITIONS & CONDITIONS

note: *there is room to shift, add to, resist, and redirect these identifications to establish emergent and adaptive consent*

map your own uses and definitions for the space in part & whole what abstract 'communications' do we collectively need to define?

possibilities include:
" I want the whole group to do something"
"I have something to tell/share with the collective"
"please stop," "that's ok," or other consent-based terms
and what else?

what would communicating this nonverbally entail?

what would a 'hard reboot' require or entail,
either individually or for the group?
what are the terms? what happens?

REFLECTING ON "INTER/FACINGS" : PROMPTS

How and why is what happened in this space available to me in other contexts, or how NOT and why NOT?

How does this experience relate to being in a public/a body / make visible how often you are actually in a public; what does it mean to treat your body as PART of a body, and how can that ripple? How can you reframe passage / experience and 'destination'?

What about this work can be applied / translated into daily experience, both public and private? how, when, where and why?

46 ||| | a score we made and used

FURTHER NOTES AND EXERCISES
FOR PROCESSES USED

SOMATIC / BREATH BASED WARM-UPS

We work with SOMATIC practices as a way to warm up, to arrive in the space, and to feel an individual and collective sense of embodiment. We will activate the Parasympathetic Nervous System (PNS), facilitate cellular respiration, and access visualization as a resource for radical thought.

Choreographer RoseAnne Spradlin writes:

"The word *soma* is defined as the body as perceived from within. To dancers, a somatic approach has come to mean loading one's performance resonance so that an audience not only sees but also feels what is in front of them. Through embodiment, the performer invites a suspension of analysis of the gifts (or deficiencies) of said dancer and instead invites an inner experience of the dancer through the phenomenon of resonance. To have a somatic experience, a member of the audience doesn't have to do anything, but rather may allow his or her body cells to focus perception on the internal as well as the external kinetic experience on view. If you feel moved when you watch a performer or a group of performers as they dance, even if you don't know what the specific movement means to you, you are likely having a somatic experience. Try letting go - try letting yourself go all the way in...and enjoy the ride."

ACTIVATING THE PARASYMPATHETIC NERVOUS SYSTEM (PNS):
4/7 BREATHWORK PRACTICE

The Parasympathetic Nervous System (PNS) encourages rest, digestion, and internal awareness. Its other key actions, as explored by Bonnie Bainbridge Cohen in her Body-Mind Centering work, are that of 'tend and befriend.' Therefore not only does this part of our nervous system allow us to locate and identify ourselves, perhaps in the midst of a chaotic or overwhelming environment, it also allows us to bridge isolation, find companionship, reach outward while still giving ourselves what we need.

To activate the PNS, inhale for 4 counts and exhale for 7 counts. Visualize this breath emanating from and returning to your heart region. Practice this breath pattern until you feel calm, open, ready.

SAMPLE SOMATIC MOVEMENT-BASED WARM-UP

This sample warm up activates systems of the body key to movement and physical investigation, from Nervous to Musculoskeletal to Lymphatic systems. The facilitator leads the warm up, provides guided imagery, and participates in the instructions themselves. Participants begin lying down in stillness, and after the 5 - 15 minute warm up they have graduated to be moving / running / standing, in action.

- Begin lying on your back if you are feeling private and inward-facing. Begin lying on your stomach if you feel open, exploratory, curious.

- I invite you to close your eyes in order to at first tune into internal sensations, but if and when you begin to move around the space you may flutter your eyes open and closed based on curiosity, and also for safety.

- I also invite you to tune me out when you need to: listen to what your body is needing, and if I move on to a specific kind of instruction or imagery that clashes with where you're at, you are welcome to continue along whatever strain of physical / mental activity you are already riding.

- As you lie on your back, tune into your breath. Notice how it falls into your chest. Can you direct it, visualize it, so that instead of just your lungs and chest pulsing your entire body breathes? How does this affect your position on the floor. Feel free to become more comfortable, shift, decide to adjust.

- As you inhale, imagine all your cells inhaling, taking in oxygen, making you more buoyant. As you exhale, visualize all your cells disseminating more water into your body, making your movements more fluid.

- Picture your lymph nodes behind your ears. You can gently massage them to locate them. How can you guide more fluid to these spaces, encourage healing, expand the reach of your lymphatic system which keeps you healthy and defends the rest of you.

- As you lie on the ground, notice how these images of fluids, which started from the breath, start to encourage movement. A rocking, a back and forth. If you find yourself rolling on the floor, maybe like a ship on a quiet sea, tap into which of your joint capsules are in contact with the floor. Visualize your exhale filling these joints up with more synovial fluid than they had before. You're making pillows for these joints. Your knees, your elbows, even the sutures in your skull which, while they don't glide or slide, are joints nonetheless.... Go with that for a little. Take yourself on a little synovial journey. And remember, if you start graduating planes and find yourself crawling or even coming to crouch or stand, you can flutter your eyes open, do what you need, explore.

• As you find fluidity in the joints, find the floor with your hands. Press your weight into them, and maybe into your feet as well, or your knees if you're in a position similar to a crawl. Or your sitz bones if you are sitting. Wherever you are, notice that contact and press your weight into the floor. Begin to lever your body off those contact points to create heat, activating our musculoskeletal systems.

• Our bones are spiralic: structurally they encourage nonlinearity, askewness, divergence, motion. They are not straight. They are not brittle: they have many layers including a spongy interior. Our muscles have two contrasting roles which work in dynamic opposition: they support and steady our skeletal system, but they also lend it mobility. Our muscles help us extend into space, stretch, collapse, expand. Play with this. Allow it to feel good. This is an internal investigation: work within your range of motion, and this is enough.

• If you find some sound trying to come out: I encourage you to go there. Sounding can be a way to physically direct your energy to a specific region or system of the body. Opening your mouth in the shape of various vowels can be a helpful place to start. (Demonstrate.)

• Continue to lever, fluttering eyes open more and more so that you are able to perceive what is around you. We are not isolated organisms in a space. We comprise an ecosystem. There are others of us, with us, moving near us. Here we move into a sort of toggling: between the parasympathetic nervous system, which helps us rest and digest, and the sympathetic nervous system, which empowers us to reach outward, assess our environment, act, run. Eye contact can be a helpful practice to continue to expand in your movement as you start tapping into your nervous system in this way.

• Allow this toggling to become literal, physical. To reach inward, and play inside your internal landscape, maybe you slow down, maybe you go back into the lowest plane of the floor. To reach outward, maybe you notice an area or aspect of the space that you feel curious about and move toward it. Seek something out. Become curious and follow that curiosity. (Demonstrate.)

- Now we're moving together. We are in concert, while still maintaining our own systems investigation and personal warm up. We are creating a space together, moving with each other, seeing one another. It's ok to smile at your neighbor...

- Settle where you are, stay standing or wherever your body is or needs to be, and let your eyes close. Notice your breathing. Notice your joints. Notice where you've created heat. Just notice that, and when you're ready we will come together.

This warm up was influenced by workshops taught by KJ Holmes, Mina Nishimura, Juliette Mapp, Ni'Ja Whitson, and Neil Greenberg, held at Movement Research in New York City.

SEE RESOURCES FOR FURTHER / RELEVANT READING / FURTHER EXERCISES

Cohen, Bonnie Bainbridge, Lisa Nelson, and Nancy Stark Smith. *Sensing, Feeling, and Action: The Experiential Anatomy of Body-Mind Centering®*. Third edition. Northampton, MA: Contact Editions, 2012.

Spradlin, RoseAnne. "Context Notes for 'Y.'" New York Live Arts, 2018.

REPETITIONS AND OBSERVATIONS EXERCISE

This exercise draws loosely on the method of actor training developed by Sanford Meisner to help actors actively listen to their scene partners and respond honestly, and spontaneously, in the moment. In adapting the approach for use outside of an acting studio, we are most interested in encouraging workshop participants to de-program their habits of listening, observing, and interpreting.

PART I: For 15 minutes, partners observe one another and write down as many true observations as possible. The observation/writing is done simultaneously—both partners are writing at the same time. The writing will not be shown to anyone, and should be as comprehensive as possible; it should include observations about perceived thoughts/emotions, and speculative observations about occupation, background, sexuality, etc. The goal (but this is not explained in advance to participants) is that this experience is recursive: in actively trying to interpret nonverbal cues and name the assumptions to which they give rise, participants imagine and consider what their partner might be writing/interpreting about them. The exercise leader might give some instruction: for example, begin sitting; after five minutes, ask partner A to walk back and forth across the space, then partner B; etc.

PART II: For 10 minutes, do basic, "objective" repetitions (commenting on clothing, physical movements, etc.), maintaining unbroken eye contact. Have participants try to imagine what their partner wrote about them in Part I as they do these repetitions. Give the instruction "invent nothing, deny nothing" (that's from David Mamet). Model repetitions first for participants. It will go something like this:

> A: Your shirt is red.
> B: My shirt is red.
> A: Your shirt is red.
> B: My shirt is red.
> A: Your shirt is red.
> B: My shirt is red.
> A: Your shirt is red.
> B: You scratched your nose.
> A: I scratched my nose.
> B: You scratched your nose.

A: I scratched my nose.
B: You scratched your nose.
A: Your shoe is untied.
B: My shoe is untied.
A: Your shoe is untied.
B: My shoe is untied.
A: Your shoe is untied. [etc.].

If you wish, you can then model "subjective" repetitions. These are closer to what actors would be doing when learning the building blocks of the Meisner technique. We recommend, in a brief workshop, not actually asking participants to do this sort of repetition; it's a vulnerable experience, and the goal of enabling apparently naturalistic, spontaneous responses onstage (i.e. in a fictionalized environment) isn't (in our view) relevant to precarity work.

After repetitions, participants freewrite for 3-5 minutes.

PART III: For 7 minutes, without writing anything or speaking, partners maintain unbroken eye contact while sitting or standing in a neutral comfortable position. Participants are instructed to let go of the actions of observing, judging, and interpreting with which they were tasked in Parts I and II.

Then, for 3-5 minutes, participants talk with their partners about the entire exercise.

FURTHER/RELEVANT READING:

Meisner, Sanford, Dennis Longwell, and Sydney Pollack. Sanford Meisner On Acting. New York: Random House, 1987.
Goffman, Erving. The Presentation of Self in Everyday Life. New York: Doubleday, 1959.

OTHER THEATRE ARTISTS TO MINE FOR EXERCISES FOR PRECARITY WORK:

Boal, Augusto. Games for Actors and Non-Actors. 2nd ed. New York: Routledge, 2002.
———. Legislative Theatre: Using Performance to Make Politics. London ; New York: Routledge, 1998.
———. Theater of the Oppressed. New York: Urizen Books, 1979.
Bogart, Anne, and Tina Landau. The Viewpoints Book: A Practical Guide

to *Viewpoints and Composition*. 1st ed edition. New York : St. Paul, MN: Theatre Communications Group, 2004.

Carson, Jo. Spider *Speculations: A Physics and Biophysics of Storytelling*. New York: Theatre Communications Group, 2006.

"Cornerstone Theater Company - About." Accessed January 8, 2019. https://cornerstonetheater.org/about/. Key player and longtime maker of work in community-based theater; formerly itinerant, now based in Los Angeles. Hosts Summer Institutes and other training programs.

"About." Junebug Productions. Accessed January 8, 2019. https://junebugproductions.org/about/. Organizational successor to the Free Southern Theater, a major influence on the Black Arts Movement and originator of the story circles method.

Spolin, Viola. *Improvisation for the Theater: A Handbook of Teaching and Directing Techniques*. 3 edition. Evanston, Ill: Northwestern University Press, 1999.

AUTHENTIC MOVEMENT FRAMEWORK / EXERCISE

Authentic Movement (AM) is a partnered movement and witnessing practice. First created by Mary Starks Whitehouse, AM can inform the choreographic process, serve as a warm up, or work as a tool to (re)pattern and (re)explore how we move. Budwig first practiced Authentic Movement under choreographer and practitioner DD Dorvillier.

In one of Dorvillier's recent workshop descriptions, she describes it as:

"A simple premise of spending an active or not-so-active period of time with eyes closed while being observed by a partner, combined with a simple premise of spending a somewhat still period of time with eyes open while observing a partner in action, moving and/or making sound, or not. The participants have the opportunity to direct and follow their own learning and self-reflection both in movement and in the witnessing of others moving. In our workshop, stormy relies on this practice to encourage deep listening, offer a method to dive into and out of assumption and narrative, and provide a deeply healing way to inhabit one's body in solitude and together."

FURTHER/RELEVANT READING:

Dorvillier, DD. "Moving with Eyes Closed (AKA Authentic Movement)." ImPulsTanz Festival Workshop Archive 2015, n.d. https://www.impulstanz.com/en/archive/2015/workshops/id2811/.
Joy, Jenn. "Anatomies of Spasm." In *The Choreographic*. Cambridge, Massachusetts: The MIT Press, 2014.
Whitehouse, Mary Starks, Janet Adler, Joan Chodorow, and Patrizia Pallaro. *Authentic Movement*. London: Philadelphia : J. Kingsley Publishers, 1999.

ADDITIONAL NOTES ON USING OUR SCORE

A NOTE IN OPENING:

If you were to run this score independently of this workshop framework, you might consider adding a short introductory reading (read aloud) or other media to jump off from to add some context. Every iteration of this score will be entirely unique, and framing within / in response to texts or other materials would in turn influence each performance / iteration. In this case, the framework is already the overarching questions of precarity and somatics, etc., but other frameworks / workshop environments could imbue its practices with deeply meaningful insights around other aspects of human experience and interaction.

IN COMPOSING THIS SCORE WE ASKED OURSELVES:

- What do we hope gets worked out in the group through the performance of the score?
- What about this work can be applied / translated into quotidian experience both in:re private and public?
- What former parts of the workshop, if any, would we build into or build onto through the score? Movement, somatic awareness, breathing, observation, listening, identifying/writing/languaging, expressing, responsiveness, adaptation, eye contact
- How do we establish and/or build on the relationship we have begun to create with each other in and also with the space itself?

We were interested in the ways in which the score could trouble each participant's relationship to boundaries and the intersection of the public and private and particularly in terms of consent: how to recognise, be aware of and be responsive to the bodies, language, and needs of others while also learning how to create discrete distinction between the self / private and the public when the body / mind / spirit requires it or would be served by it.

The score as composed asks each participant to both watch, observe, respond or react or make eye contact and/or touch or connect but also discipline, assert, move away from, protect, distinguish, find quiet / distance, and require consent, in ways that built on the somatic, movement, writing, self-analysis, and other exercises our workshop had already sketched out, using emergent gesture and signal co-created by the group.

SAMPLE SCORE PARAMETERS AS USED

INTRO / FRAMING
[*Suggested duration: 15 minutes*]

Invite participants into the score environment by explaining the framework of the score, how the group will collectively establish and use terms and signals, etc. Read framing / prompt text if desired. We chose not to talk about intended applications or potential take-aways of the experience until after; you may want to include some specific applications in your case.

ESTABLISHING TERMS & ABSTRACT MOVEMENTS
[*Suggested duration: 35 minutes*]

Mapping use and identification of the space (privately, then physically)
Individual brainstorm about site / space definitions / prescriptions
Mapping with tape and/or post-its

Have group collectively identify:
Abstracted movements that convey: I want the whole group to do something, I have something to tell everyone, etc.
Establish a hard reboot - what are the terms, what happens?

Have participants Identify / brainstorm (individually, written):
spatial definitions / prescriptions / rules
1 thing each personally wants to do (private want)
1 thing each wants other individuals to do (interpersonal want)
1 thing each wants other people to do as a group (public want)

RUN SCORE
[*Suggested duration: minimum 1hr*]

Notes: A "go" and a "hard reboot" are set collectively by the group or by facilitator as desired. We allowed three hard reboots in our session.

END SCORE: use timer to signal 10 minutes to end
[*Suggested duration: 10 minute easing out*]

REFLECTIONS / OBSERVATIONS
[*Suggested duration: 15 minutes*]

Allow participants time to quietly reflect and write before group discussion. Discussion of application, insights will depend on framework.

SCORES & INSTRUCTIONS TO USE AND EXPLORE

Here we're using the term 'score' (as explained in our definitions) as an overarching term to describe not only complete, written compositions with a discrete beginning and end but rather, a category of instruction / rule based performance / experience / experimental practices for one or more persons that reframe positionality within space, place, interaction, and human experience in general.

Since we are thinking about somatic practices in particular, for our purposes written exercises like poet CA Conrad's Somatic Poetics prompts fit comfortably under this umbrella, while other less explicitly body-oriented written experimentation, visual rule-based instructions /experimentations or sound/music based experimental scores might seem less suited. However, all of these 'scored' environments share a common purpose: to re-orient the body, the senses, and our conditioned perceptions, producing as a result any range of media which our training has a tendency to block. Not surprisingly, there can also be a lot of overlap between "scores" and mindfulness meditations, reframing self-awareness in space. Self-hacking, indeed.

We thoroughly encourage you to explore and use instruction based practices across media you currently are familiar with in your pratice, as well as (and perhaps, in particular) ones that fall outside your usual process and set of materials / comfort zone.

We've put together a sample set of procedures / scores / instructions here, but many many more can be found in the resources listed at the end of this section and in our bibliographic resource section.

SNOW PIECE

Think that snow is falling. Think that snow is falling
everywhere all the time. When you talk with a person, think
that snow is falling between you and on the person.
Stop conversing when you think the person is covered by snow.
—1963

(*Score by Yoko Ono from "AIU: Selected Instruction Pieces by Yoko Ono."*
Accessed January 7, 2019. http://www.a-i-u.net/instructions.html.)

REMOVING THE DEMON OR GETTING YOUR ROCKS OFF

Sit in a circle with persons facing in and out alternately. If the number in the group is odd, seat the left over person in the center. Each person except the center person has a pair of resonant rocks. Begin the meditation by establishing mentally a tempo as slow as possible. Each person begins independently to strike the rocks together full force maintaining the imagined tempo. When enough energy is present, shout a pre-meditated word. Once selected, the word remains the same. The shout is free of the established tempo, and may occur one or more times during the meditation. The center person is without rocks and selects a word, phrase or sentence to say or intone repeatedly either silently or audibly for the duration of the meditation.

Variations:

a) Persons without rocks may surround the circle and follow the some instructions as the center person, independently.
b) Persons may repeat mentally, or actually, one body movement as slowly as possible .. One body movement may be simple or very complicated as long as It is continuous and can be repeated exactly as a cycle. Kinetic participants could include the shout or the repeated word, phrase or sentence.
c) Do this meditation in an outdoor environment. Move slowly away from the circle. Move anywhere in the environment but keep in audible contact with at least one other person. Gradually return to the beginning circle.

(Score by Pauline Oliveros from Sonic Meditations,
Smith Publications, 1974.)

HOMING: A SCORE FOR ONE PERFORMER

Tonight, you are not allowed to go home until you have convinced yourself that you will never go home again.

(Score by Cory Tamler and Jennie Hahn from In Kinship, 2015,
http://www.open-waters.org/performancescores/.)

A SCORE BASED ON TRANSFORMATION, RESISTANCE, AND GROUP ACTION

i) Everyone in the space is rolling slowly around. If someone chooses to stand everyone pauses to look at them. If someone starts crawling, everyone gradually joins to crawl in their same direction. Water is in the center of the space. If you take a water break, there's an option to chat &

hang out. There is an option for a person who stands to teach the group something —a repetitive loop or series of movements— that everyone has the choice of learning / doing together or not...That fades out when it feels like it. Every hour on the hour everyone gets up and goes outside to stand together in silence to get some fresh air and listen to the trees. After four hours of this there's an assembly for thirty minutes in which everyone decides how to do something or change something about the score.

(*Score by storm budwig*)

TIMES SQUARE INTERVENTION

Situate yourself* centrally in the center of Times Square in New York City at a busy time of day so that you are surrounded by billboards, lights, and people on all sides. How does this make you feel? Do you avoid this space or place? How do you react to the people here? Allow your ordinary reaction to grow within you. Check in with your pulse, your breath, your muscles, your jaw: where are you holding tension? Is your breath shallow or your pulse elevated? Do you experience frustration or a desire to avoid this experience or cast judgement on the strangers who surround you?

Close your eyes and breathe deeply. You have nowhere to go. Rushing is a condition of the scarcity of time, and you are a being of ease and grace. Allow your breath and body to settle. Give your arms a little shake and roll your head side to side, slowly.

With your eyes still closed, imagine that you are in a vast canyon, one of earth's natural wonders. Without opening your eyes, sense that above you is the sky, coming in through the top of this high canyon. Feel its height to your sides. Around you, feel the pulsing of the hive of your biome: the humans, the buildings, the pigeons, the air, your body, all made of the same materials. All a canyon of human making and yearning. Breathe slowly and deeply, and imagine your edges blurring, so that you and this space and its trappings are indistinguishable.

Open your eyes and see the canyon. Can you see the people around you or this place with the eyes of a child, full of wonderment? Can you feel compassion towards your species and its endearing urge to reach for the sky, to compete with the trees and mountains? Breathe here, feeling your new eyes, your solidity on the ground, the schist below.

[*You may perform this score either on site or as a visualization practice. If the latter, close your eyes, center with a few sets of deep breaths, and imagine yourself following the instructions as if on site.]

(*score by Elæ Moss*)

67 // MAP SCORE

Find as many historical maps as possible of a lost ecology.

Trace these maps.

Layer these maps on a contemporary map.

Worry about the accuracy of where you have placed the maps.

Don't worry about the accuracy of where you have placed the maps.

Consider the false sense of objectivity in the contemporary map.

Add maps of recent environmental events.

Look at the map through your discipline's eyes, then through the eyes of your collaborators' disciplines.

Imagine the place through the eyes of city dwellers in the past.

Imagine the place through the eyes of those who made the historical maps.

Walk the map.

> (*iLANDing Laboratory, 2015. "Collect Pond: The Urban Backstage." in* A Field Guide to iLANDing, *53rd State Press, 2017.*)

(SOMA)TIC 5: STORM SOAKED BREAD

Sit outside under shelter of a doorway, pavilion, or umbrella on a park bench, but somewhere outside where you can easily touch, smell, taste, FEEL the storm. Lean your face into the weather, face pointed UP to the sky, stay there for a bit with eyes closed while water fills the wells of your eyes. Come back into the shelter properly baptized in the beauty of pure elements and be quiet and still for a few minutes. Take some preliminary notes about your surroundings. Try not to engage with others who might run to your shelter for cover. If they insist on talking MOVE somewhere else; you are a poet with a storm to digest, this isn't time for small talk! You are not running from the storm, you are opening to it, you are IN IT! Stick a bare arm or foot into the storm, let your skin take in a meditative measure of wind and rain. If you are someone who RAN from storms in the past take time to examine the joys of the experience. Remind yourself you are a human being who is approximately 80 percent water SO WHAT'S THE

HARM OF A FEW DROPS ON THE OUTSIDE!? Right? YES! Pause, hold your breath for a count of 4, then write with a FURY and without thinking, just let it FLOW OUT OF YOU, write, write, WRITE!

Set an empty cup in the storm, hold a slic of bread in the storm. Then put a little salt and pepper on your storm soaked bread, maybe some oregano and garlic. With deliberate SLOOOWNESS chew your storm bread and drink the storm captured in your cup. Slowly. So, slowly, please, with, a, slowness, that, is, foreign, to, you. THINK the whole slow time of chewing and drinking how this water has been in a cycle for MILLIONS OF YEARS, falling to earth, quenching horses, elephants, lizards, dinosaurs, humans. They pissed, they died, their water evaporated and gathered again into clouds to drizzle down AND STORM DOWN into rivers, puddles, aqueducts, and ancient cupped hands. Humans who LOVED, who are long dead, humans who thieved, raped, murdered, were generous, playful, disappointed, fearful, annoyed and adored one another, each of them dying in their own way, their water going back to the sky, coming back down to your bread, your lips, your stomach, to feed your sinew, your brain, your living, beautiful day. Take your notes POET, IT IS YOUR MOMENT to be totally aware, completely aware!

(CA Conrad, from A Beautiful Marsupial Afternoon:
New (Soma)tics. Wave Books, 2012.)

FURTHER/RELEVANT READING:

Kliën, Michael. "Excavation Sites & Phenomenological Learning Environments," 2014, 8. http://www.michaelklien.com/resource/download/excavation-sites2014.pdf.

Laboratory for Art Nature Dance, Interdisciplinary. A Field Guide to ILanding: Research Scores for Urban Ecologies. Brooklyn, NY: 53rd State Press, 2017.

Lazier, Rebecca, and Dan Trueman. There Might Be Others, 2016.

Oliveros, Pauline. On Sonic Meditation. La Jolla, Ca.: Center for Music Experiment and Related Research, University of California at San Diego, 1973.

Ono, Yōko. Grapefruit: A Book of Instructions. London: Owen, 1970.

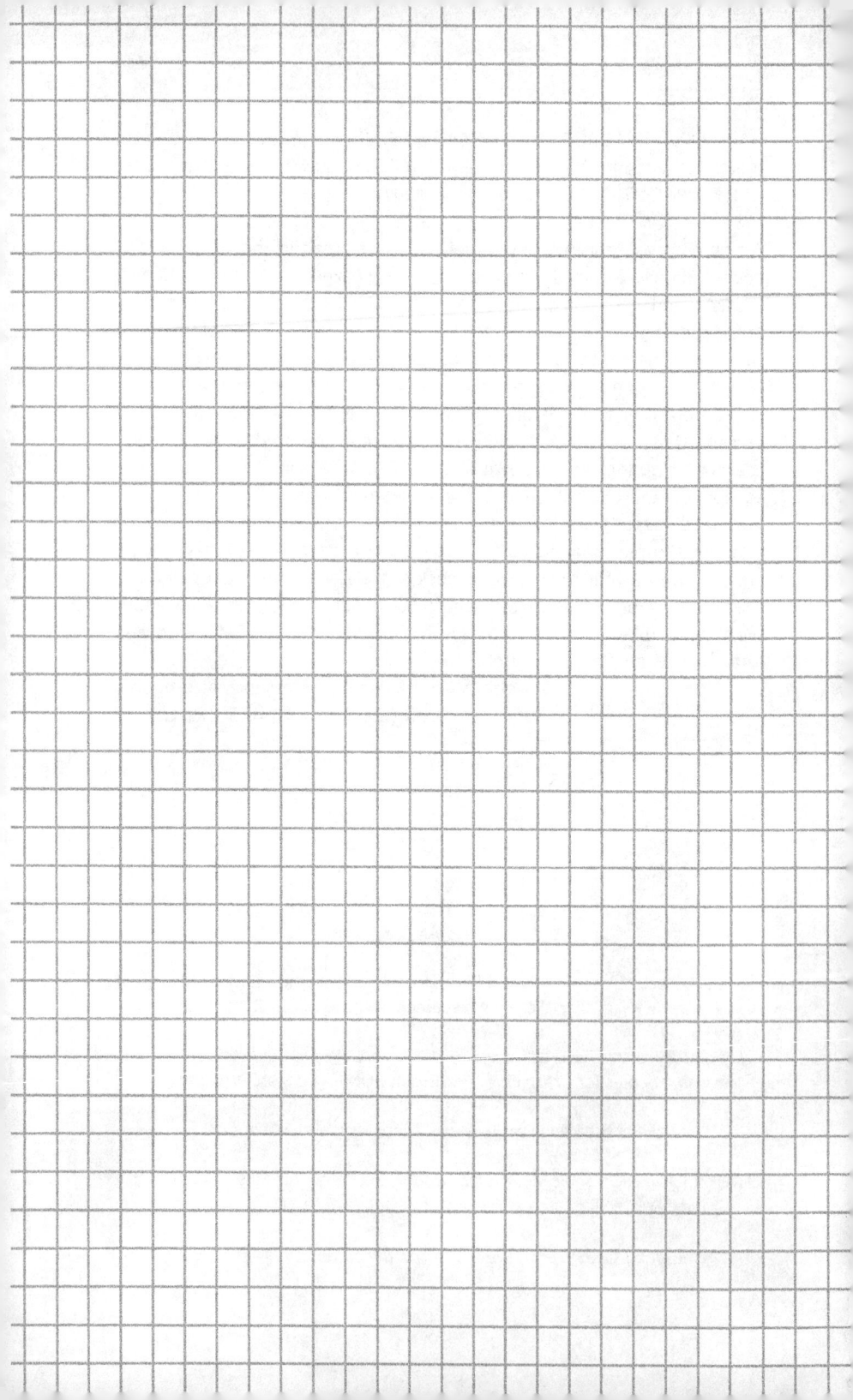

FURTHER RESOURCES to USE AND EXPLORE

Please note: this is a collective bibliography. A good number of these resources are at play in all of our practices in different ways, and we've chosen not to credit our annotations. It's important to mention, though, that the following weren't annotated by the people you necessarily assume! We are all working interdisciplinarily, which means that Elæ provided and annotated many entries on dance or performance, stormy and Cory on theory, and so on, as well as work from "our" fields.

Adams, Rachel, David Serlin, and Benjamin Reiss. *Keywords for Disability Studies* .New York: NYU Press, 2015. Web extension with teaching guides and sample texts at https://keywords. nyupress.org/disability-studies/

> For anyone considering how all bodies move through and are operated upon by spaces, places, and others, entrance into disability studies is essential. These 60 critical concept essays on topics such as "ethics," "normal," "stigma," "performance," etc, approach disability "as an embodied condition, a mutable historical phenomenon, and a social, political, and cultural identity."

Ahmed, Sara. *Living a Feminist Life*. Durham: Duke University Press, 2017.

> Annotation (stormy): Sara Ahmed's Living a Feminist Life is an exemplary model of intersectionality that helps bridge the gap between work done inside a closed loop (like a workshop) and work done in the everyday. Ahmed shows that how we exist together and respond to one another does not have to be limited to what society imposes on us. Rather, we can establish new connections and new protocols for relation that are more humane and equitable. This text can be viewed as both infrastructure and outcome of consciousness raising work.

———. *Queer Phenomenology: Orientations, Objects, Others*. Durham: Duke University Press, 2006.

> Taking up the concept of orientation (with its sexual, but also, prominently, its spatial connotations) to bring queer studies and phenomenology into conversation with one another, Ahmed asks what meaning is made by our orientation towards particular objects. Orientation towards objects is connected to presence, and this

presence defines what we perceive as being possible—the options that are available to us. Presence is, however, not enough; an object may be within reach, but that does not mean we will reach for it. Ahmed articulates this understanding of the body in space through lines that connect bodies and things, allowing us to find our way but also constricting what is available to us. She begins by approaching a definition of orientation through phenomenology in her first chapter, which she then queers in Chapter 2. Her final chapter brings the racialization of space into her argument. Arguing that bodies and objects tend towards one another in the sense that objects are formed for particular bodies, she draws a line connecting action with space in a two-way relationship; we don't just act in space, but "spatial relations between subjects and others are produced through actions, which make some things available to be reached" (52). Our actions produce space and space shapes our bodies. Though Ahmed's analysis is often tied to the intimate, seemingly the private sphere, this interconnectedness and mutual shaping of bodies/spaces ("for women to claim a space to write is a political act" (61)) shows the way that the private and the public must necessarily bleed into one another. The familiar mantra "the personal is political" could be reformulated "the private is public".

Barad, Karen Michelle. *Meeting the Universe Halfway: Quantum Physics and the Entanglement of Matter and Meaning.* Durham: Duke University Press, 2007.

> Barad's book is an impressive achievement, functioning as a cross-disciplinary work of science studies, critical theory, theoretical physics, ontological studies, and more. In its pages she develops her theory of agential realism, which draws on Niels Bohr's interpretation of quantum physics to understand how an apparatus (of measurement) not only affects, but is affected by, that which it measures. Agential realism is a powerful theory that can be used to talk about how beings and things are networked, and how they create one another through what she terms intra-action.

Bartky, Sandra. *Femininity and Domination: Studies in the Phenomenology of Oppression.* New York: Routledge, 1990.

> Sandra Bartky calls, in these theoretical essays, for "a political phenomenology of the emotions" that would analyze emotions for the way they are sociopolitically

constructed, remedying a Marxist tendency to under-theorize individual experience in combating ideology. This imperative, to understand and politically/critically mobilize "the ways in which the social and economic tensions [...] are played out in the lives of concrete individuals," remains at the heart of much feminist and queer theory and activism. Bartky on false needs, Bartky on consciousness-raising, Bartky on desire, Bartky on shame—it's all delicious.

Bass, Chloë. *The Book of Everyday Instruction*. The Operating System, 2018.

From 2015-18, New York based social practice artist Chloë Bass engaged in a question-driven series of interdisciplinary experiments and processes around social interactions, posing deceivingly simple queries such as "how do we know if we're really together?","do we invent the people we love?" and "what is the story told by the distance between two bodies in space?" Exploring intimacy, language, identity, perception, belonging, and place, and sited in various cities around the US, this book brings together eight project "chapters," gathering both the process materials as well as documentation of installation and public engagement, alongside critical texts.

Basśo, Keith Hamilton. *Wisdom Sits in Places: Landscape and Language among the Western Apache*. Albuquerque: Univ. of New Mexico Press, 2010.

In our engagement with the body in place, we must not lose track of how culturally specific / conditioned this relationship can be, even when it feels "natural." Basso's fieldwork with the Western Apache in Arizona engages the reader in the perceptual landscape and interior worldview of another embodied reality palimpsestically co-existent in the country now defined as the "United States," via the narrative language of place and place names of the indigenous tradition.

Baudrillard, Jean. *Simulacra and Simulation*. Ann Arbor: University of Michigan Press, 1994.

A gateway drug into self-hacking through philosophy, this 1981 postmodern classic from French philosopher Jean Baudrillard re-presents our perceptual, lived hyper-"reality" as in fact a simulacra, framing ours as an image-saturated, language-and-ideology-mediated experience which bears no resemblance to an actual "real," where "the map precedes the territory." For the body / human seeking to negotiate and identify where their perceptions / readings of the "real" begin and end, start with the first essay, "The Precession of Simulacra," widely available as a pdf.

Berlant, Lauren. *Cruel Optimism*. Duke University Press, 2011.

———."Affect is the New Trauma," in *The Critical Pulse: Thirty-Six Credos by Contemporary Critics*. 2012.

Bishop, Claire. *Artificial Hells: Participatory Art and the Politics of Spectatorship*. New York: Verso, 2014.

Bishop, an art critic and historian, attempts to develop a critical aesthetic framework for talking about participatory art. In so doing, she points out art's co-optation within a neoliberal framework to fulfill functions and offer services in place of the state, shifting responsibility for social services to the artist.

Boal, Augusto. *Games for Actors and Non-Actors*. 2nd ed. New York: Routledge, 2002.

———. Legislative Theatre: Using Performance to Make Politics. London ; New York: Routledge, 1998.

———. Theater of the Oppressed. New York: Urizen Books, 1979.

Collected under the umbrella term "Theatre of the Oppressed," the technique of Brazilian theatre artist, activist, and politician Augusto Boal is widely drawn on to help oppressed communities identify the oppressive structures and forces that act on them and to rehearse (in a dialectical, non-prescriptive fashion) potential solutions. In a TO performance there are no performers or audience, but "spect-actors," all of whom are able to step into the performance and try out tactics to change the situation. Boal was in regular dialogue with Freire (Pedagogy of the Oppressed) and uses a great deal of Freire's thinking and pedagogical approach.

Bogart, Anne, and Tina Landau. *The Viewpoints Book: A Practical Guide to Viewpoints and Composition*. 1st ed edition. New York : St. Paul, MN: Theatre Communications Group, 2004.

Brecht, Bertolt. Brecht on Theatre: The Development of an Aesthetic. Edited by Steve Giles, Marc Silberman, and Tom Kuhn. Translated by John Willett. 13th edition. London u.a: Hill and Wang, 1977.

———. *Measures Taken and Other Lehrstucke*. Edited by Ralph Manheim. Translated by Carl R. Mueller and Wolfgang Sauerlander. Translation edition. London: Methuen Drama, 2006.

When it comes to overturning power structures and inciting revolution, German Marxist director and playwright Brecht's theory is bigger than his practice (which tends to turn didactic even as it argues for an audience of critical thinkers). But his approach to alienation is relevant to this work, as a way in to understanding how a Marxist concept of alienation might be approached through embodiment. Neither audience nor performers should identify with the characters portrayed onstage, creating distance between the story and its observers/agents that makes visible how strange the systems of capitalism are. This estrangement (often considered a better translation of Verfremdungseffekt than "alienation effect") is meant to provoke thought, argument, a desire for change, and action. Brecht's Lehrstuecke, or teaching plays, are plays performed without an audience; in reading and discussing the plays, everyone in the room should have to think through the puzzle and arrive at their own answer.

brown, adrienne m. *Emergent Strategy*. Chico, CA: AK Press, 2017.

> Annotation: adrienne maree brown's Emergent Strategy is a point of departure for organizers. It is also offers sharp left turns, fresh starts, and case by case tools for those already involved in a lengthy project. A central concept stormy takes from this text whenever she teaches a workshop is the vital importance of arriving together, and of listening deeply to what arises in and of the room.

Burroughs, Jonathan. "Keynote Address for the Postdance Conference in Stockholm, Sweden." In *Contemporary Choreography: A Critical Reader*, edited by Jo Butterworth and Liesbeth Wildschut, Second edition. Milton Park, Abingdon, Oxon ; New York, NY: Routledge, 2017.

> Annotation: A rally cry for (dance-)makers wondering about lineage, the contemporary, and belonging to a community that is transient, pluralistic, and impossible to define.

Butler, Judith. *Notes toward a Performative Theory of Assembly*. Cambridge, Massachusetts: Harvard University Press, 2015.

———. *Precarious Life: The Powers of Mourning and Violence*. London: Verso, 2006.

> Judith Butler's recent work has dealt specifically with precarity and how it affects our ability to assemble and protest, to grieve, and to come together. Rooted in the body and what the collective body says without speaking, Butler's writing on precarity and assembly traces a new, contemporary way of understanding what it means to form a public.

Cameron, Julia. *The Artist's Way: A Spiritual Path to Higher Creativity*, 2016.

> Too frequently we divide our attentions between the texts and works that 'belong' in academic and professional bibliographies, and those that circulate widely in our creative and broader communities. At the intersection of grappling with identity, creative practice, possibility, and precarity, especially vis-a-vis questions of agency and permission, there's almost always someone I know using The Artist's Way - a classic "self-help" best seller from Julia Cameron which opens the reader / user up to their own blocks, self-perceptions, fears, etc., around creative practice, and offers prompts, tools, and rituals to re-envigorate (or start) a practice. A newer volume exists, It's Never Too Late to Begin Again, specifically for those self-hacking into a new identity in midlife. The process of using a book like this can be profound. Her morning pages have been something many return to again and again.

Carson, Jo. *Spider Speculations: A Physics and Biophysics of Storytelling*. New York: Theatre Communications Group, 2006.

> "I've spent about 15 years plus some working with people's stories in a series of communities in this country. I write plays from oral histories for those communities. Just finished my 30th. I'm watching people's lives and communities literally change, sometimes drastically, for the work. Spider Speculations is the beginning of trying to understand the hows and whys of all the changes." —Jo Carson

Certeau, Michel de. *The Practice of Everyday Life*. [1] [1. Berkeley, Calif.: Univ. of California Press, 2008.

Chödrön, Pema. *Taking the Leap: Freeing Ourselves from Old Habits and Fears.* S.l.: SHAMBHALA, 2019.

———. *When Things Fall Apart: Heart Advice for Difficult Times*, 2017.

———, cloudLibrary, and TEST. *Natural Awareness Guided Meditations and Teachings for Welcoming All Experience.* S.l.: Sounds True Audio, 2012.

———, and Emily Hilburn Sell. *Comfortable with Uncertainty*: 108 Teachings, 2018.

> Following in the footsteps on the notes for The Artist's Way, American Tibetan Buddhist nun Pema Chödrön's books are the sort of well-worn self-help go-to's that circulate in communities of collective, interpersonal healing. These practical, deceivingly

simple, compassionate and non-judgemental books provide strategies and frameworks with and within which to evaluate, address, and work through your most difficult situations, feelings, and reactions. Teachings and audio are widely available.

Cohen, Bonnie Bainbridge, Lisa Nelson, and Nancy Stark Smith. *Sensing, Feeling, and Action: The Experiential Anatomy of Body-Mind Centering®*. Third edition. Northampton, MA: Contact Editions, 2012. [See notes in Further Exercises section.]

Conrad, C. A. *A Beautiful Marsupial Afternoon: New (Soma)tics*

———.*Ecodeviance: (Soma)Tics for the Future Wilderness*, 2014.

———. *While Standing in Line for Death*, 2017.

CA Conrad is committed both in life and creative practice (if there ever were a line) to the performance and documentation of what he calls (Soma)tic poetry exercises, a series of instruction based operations by which he constrains the conditions of his body and its perception as well as the objects and space around him. He publishes both the prompts and the results of running the experience through a series of "filters." http://writing.upenn.edu/~taransky/somatic-exercises.pdf [also appears in the Scores section.]

De la Rosa, Ralph. *The Monkey Is the Messenger: Meditation and What Your Busy Mind Is Trying to Tell You*, 2018.

There's so many books on the power and efficacy of meditation for trauma and general self-hacking, but few blend neuroscience, somatics, and contemporary thinking around trauma treatment with the more commonplace mindfulness language around taming the 'monkey mind.' De la Rosa brings his training in Trauma Focused Cognitive Behavior Therapy and Internal Family Systems theory alongside many years of Buddhist and mindfulness study to this immediately applicable, valuable text.

Delany, Samuel R. *Times Square Red, Times Square Blue*. NYU Press, 1999.

A book in two essays. The first is Delany's love letter to Times Square before it was "cleaned up," an argument for the necessity of cross-class contact and sexual free space, especially for gay men. The anti-privatization argument inherent in Delany's twin pieces is worth considering in the context of precarity, as well as the plea for networks of emotional/physical support beyond the nuclear family.

DeSilva-Johnson, Lynne [Elæ Moss] "And I in the Middle Ground Found: Documentation as Self-hack, Sigil, and Blueprint." in *Matters of Feminist Practice*, Belladonna*, forthcoming 2019.

———, "Elegy for the Almost Gone: Termination Codon," in *Big Echo,* 2017. at http://www.bigecho.org/elegy-for-the-almost-gone

———, "In Memory of Feasible Grace," a Panthalassa Pamphlet, 2017. available at https://bit.ly/feasiblegrace

Dorvillier, DD. "Moving with Eyes Closed (AKA Authentic Movement)." ImPulsTanz Festival Workshop Archive 2015, n.d. https://www.impulstanz.com/en/archive/2015/workshops/id2811/.

Federici, Silvia. *Caliban and the Witch*. New York: Autonomedia, 2014.

———, George Caffentzis."Notes on the edu-factory and cognitive capitalism," http://eipcp.net/transversal/0809/caffentzisfederici/en

———, "The Body, Capitalist Accumulation And The Accumulation Of Labour Power," 2007.

Audio: http://www.brh.org.uk/brhw2007/witches3.html

Federici's thinking on the shift to capital accumulation in relationship to the body is largely familiar to those approaching the work from a specifically feminist orientation but in fact this radical scholar's thinking can provide anyone interested in re-considering the impact of capitalism and privatization of property, and the move away from a commons, on the body both individual and collective. Essential for any study of precarity in relationship to capital labor and accumulation. Her work is widely available as open source articles online.

Feenstra, Eliot. "Why does everyone I know feel so anxious? Hosting precarity consciousness-raising circles. A score for performance." 2018. Contact eliot.feenstra@gmail.com

Feldenkrais, Moshé. *Awareness through Movement: Health Exercises for Personal Growth*. Illustrated ed. New York: Harper & Row, 1977.

The Feldenkrais Method is perhaps familiar to some beyond the movement arts and within self-help / healing / mindfulness communities, but it's incredibly productive for any one thinking through this work to not only take a Feldenkrais workshop and/or work with a practitioner but also to read Feldenkrais's theoretical underpinnings for the method -- a thinking grounded in the difference between human learning and animal learning, a framework that can be enormously productive in the consideration and re-configuration of the body as a waystation for conditioned perception.

Freire, Paulo, Myra Bergman Ramos, Donaldo P Macedo, and Ira Shor.

Pedagogy of the oppressed, 2018.

> Working for many years to increase the rate of literacy in Brazil, Freire developed an approach described in this book that provides an alternative to the "banking" model of education. Freire's model puts the student (generally a working-class adult on the underside of the dominant power structure) on a plane equal to the instructor, making use of symbols and tropes meaningful to the community as the basis for learning and the development of critical thought. Freire's work was deeply influential for Augusto Boal in developing his Theatre of the Oppressed, and the two were in dialogue with one another.

Gins, Madeline, and Arakawa. *Architectural Body*. Tuscaloosa: University of Alabama Press, 2002.

> Architect Shusaku Arakawa and poet Madeline Gins collaborated for many years on the development and implementation of 'Procedural Architecture,' a process by which the 'organism-that-persons' would continue to 'learn not die,' as opposed to the normative, latter, relationship to passive pre-defined spaces of consumption and prescripted activity. The pair believed spaces could be designed to re-orient the body to its original intentions of constant adaptive learning and evolution, crystallized as the possibility of "reversible destiny." Architectural Body is the pair's manifesto. Extensive information, links, etc. can be found at http://www.reversibledestiny.org

Grosz, Elizabeth. Space, *Time and Perversion Essays on the Politics of Bodies*.Florence: Routledge, 2018. http://public.eblib.com/choice/PublicFullRecord.aspx?p=5582582.

Halprin, Anna, Siegmar Gerken, and Anna Halprin. *Returning to Health: With Dance, Movement and Imagery*. Mendocino, Calif: LifeRhythm Books, 2002. [also: *Moving Toward Life, Experience as Dance, Spirit of Place, etc.*]

> With a career beginning in the late 1930's, spanning nearly a century, Anna Halprin has consistently challenged the status quo vis-a-vis what dance can do and who it can do it for and how. Her work asks questions of the human condition, social and cultural and planetary issues and crises, healing from trauma, illness and disease, and environmental / site awareness, in this last case through collaborations with her husband, landscape architect Lawrence Halprin. Endless thinking and examples of community practice and personal work to mine.

Hanna, Thomas. *Somatics: Reawakening the Mind's Control of Movement, Flexibility, and Health*. Cambridge, MA: Da Capo Life Long, 1988.

Haraway, Donna Jeanne. *Staying with the Trouble: Making Kin in the Chthulucene*, 2016.

Hewitt, Andrew. *Social Choreography: Ideology as Performance in Dance and Everyday Movement*. Durham; London: Duke University Press, 2005.

> Social choreography is an emergent term that came into simultaneous and Independent use by Hewitt and by choreographer/artist/dramaturg duo Michael Kliën and Steve Valk. Hewitt's book marries dance theory and critical theory to argue that ideology must be seen as something that plays out in the body.

Ingold, Tim. *Being Alive: Essays on Movement, Knowledge and Description*. London; New York: Routledge, 2011.

Joy, Jenn. "Anatomies of Spasm." In *The Choreographic*. Cambridge, Massachusetts: The MIT Press, 2014.

Kimmerer, Robin Wall. *Braiding Sweetgrass*. First edition. Minneapolis, Minnesota: Milkweed Editions, 2013.

> Botanist and indigenous scientist Kimmerer writes beautifully about the kinship between human beings and the rest of the living world, a deeply necessary perspective for understanding the resources on which humans depend and which, reciprocally, depend on us.

Kliën, Michael. "Excavation Sites & Phenomenological Learning Environments," 2014. http://www.michaelklien.com/resource/download/excavation-sites2014.pdf.

> In recent years, artist and choreographer Michael Kliën has described his work as "choreographic situations," although he has also used the term "social choreography" (see Hewitt, above). Kliën creates scored situations and environments that are meant to bring participants into emergent nonverbal relationships with one another. He also considers the effect these social choreographies have on institutions (the particular concern of his collaborator Steve Valk). This work contains instructions for some of these choreographic situations, called "Excavation Sites."

Krishnamurti, J. *Commentaries on Living: Third Series, from the Notebooks of J. Krishnamurti.*, 1967.

———. *Freedom from the Known*. New York: HarperOne an Imprint of HarperCollins Publishers, 2010.

Kunst, Bojana. *Artist at Work, Proximity of Art and Capitalism*. Winchester, UK ; Washington, USA: Zero Books, 2015.

Serbian dance and theatre theorist, philosopher, and dramatist Bojana Kunst considers recent changes in artistic labor and how artistic life itself is part of the capitalist machine.

La Rocco, Claudia. "Five Attempts: Thoughts on Dance in America." In *Danse: A Catalogue*, edited by Noémie Solomon. les presses du réel new york series, 2015.

> Annotation: La Rocco contextualizes dance practice in life practice here. After given the prompt to discuss 'dance in America', the writer shows us her struggle to resist over-simplifying a complicated terrain. She shows us multiple angles and many shades. Stormy sees this resource as a helpful tool: use it to slow down your perception, take stock of the details, and to reconsider what constitutes a recognizable, characterizable thing.

Latour, Bruno. *Reassembling the Social: An Introduction to Actor-Network Theory*. Oxford: Oxford University Press, 2005.

> Latour's actor–network theory (ANT), which is broadly taken up across disciplines, represents an unusual conceptualization of spatiality that emanates from an actor (which can be human or nonhuman) rather than geographical/physical space. Latour is centrally concerned with, as his title suggests, reconnecting the social and overcoming deconstruction in its various forms. This book is divided into three parts: the first addresses the importance of retaining complexity in the social sciences, the second shows how to "render social connections traceable" (16) using ANT, and the third deals with why this is all worth pursuing. Latour frames it as a how–to manual for practitioners and by taking up this frame is performing a radical intervention with the goal of completely restructuring the way we understand social connections. Crucial is the injunction to social scientists to slow down enough that the complexity of the social is retained, and uncertainties about the nature of groups, actions, objects, and facts are not conveniently elided. ANT's world picture is relativistic, built on the acknowledgement that actors are embedded within constantly shifting networks that influence and are influenced by one another.

Laboratory for Art Nature Dance, Interdisciplinary. *A Field Guide to Ilanding: Research Scores for Urban Ecologies*. Brooklyn, NY: 53rd State Press, 2017.

> This "Field Guide" collects scores, prompts, and experiments in instruction form as well as documents

past iterations and performances from the diverse interdisciplinary collaborators over eleven years of the iLAND laboratory's work. Much more at http://www.ilandart.org. [Excerpted in Further Scores section.]

Lakoff, George, and Mark Johnson. *Philosophy in the Flesh: The Embodied Mind and Its Challenge to Western Thought*. New York: Basic Books, 1999.

> Essential introduction to the concept of embodied cognition, moving away from the enlightenment Cartesian mind-body divide towards an integrated somatic awareness in which perception, emotion, sense, body, and mind rely on and dramatically influence each other.

Lazier, Rebecca, and Dan Trueman. *There Might Be Others*, 2016.

Lepecki, André. "Limitrophies of the Human: Monstrous Nature, Thingly Life, and the Wild Animal." In *Singularities: Dance in the Age of Performance*. New York, NY: Routledge, 2016.

> A resource for those hoping to describe or put words to ineffable projects, work, and states of being. Lepecki articulates movement and embodiment here. The text is scholarly but feels like a dance. It also bridges some gaps between movement, and choreography, and dance which feel helpful when trying to understand for one's self the scope of an art practice. "Dance's understanding of the human only reflects a wider cultural-historical foundation," and as a maker / organizer / practitioner, Stormy has found this text vital to examining that reflection.

Levin, Laura, and Palgrave Macmillan. *Performing Ground: Space, Camouflage, and the Art of Blending In*. Basingstoke: Palgrave Macmillan, 2015.

> Levin's book shifts the eye to the background, the position to which space is often relegated. Her entry point is camouflage, which "contains within it an understanding of the ways that identities are negotiated in and through space" (4), thus opening up a theory of space particularly intertwined with performance. Pushing beyond the common understanding of camouflage as a temporary technique to hide the self from predators or danger, Levin's approach emphasizes camouflage as a strategy that embeds the self in its environment; it is not about disappearing, but about connecting. This approach allows camouflage to be read as the way space forms identity. Camouflage, as Levin points out, has a long history of study across disciplines;

her approach's singularity is in her interpretation of camouflage as a performance strategy. Addressing the gender blind spot in criticism of space in performance and site-specificity is another central concern.

Levine, Peter. *Waking the Tiger: Healing Trauma.* 1997.

Lipton, Bruce H. T*he Biology of Belief: 10th Anniversary Edition.* Hay House, Inc., 2016.

Macnaughton, Ian, ed. *Body, Breath & Consciousness: A Somatics Anthology: A Collection of Articles on Family Systems, Self-Psychology, the Bodynamics Model of Somatic Developmental Psychology, Shock Trauma, and Breathwork.* Berkeley, Calif: North Atlantic Books, 2004.

Malina, Judith. *Full Moon Stages: Personal Notes from 50 Years of The Living Theatre,* 2015.

Malina, Judith, Julian Beck, and N.Y. *Living Theatre* (New York. Paradise Now, Collective Creation of the Living Theatre, Written down by Judith Malina and Julian Beck.New York: Random House, 1971.

McDonough, Tom. *Guy Debord and the Situationist International: Texts and Documents.*Cambridge: MIT Press, 2004.

Morton, Timothy. *Humankind: Solidarity with Nonhuman People.* Verso, 2017.

Muñoz, José Esteban. *Disidentifications: Queers of Color and the Performance of Politics.* Minneapolis: University of Minnesota Press, 2015.

A beloved figure in performance studies, Muñoz here theorizes disidentification (a conscious act in relation to a public sphere that provides images and characters with whom the queer subaltern subject cannot fully identify, with whom fully identifying would actually mean internalizing racist or sexist ideas) as a survival technique for queers of color—one that makes possible politically powerful, radical performance.

Obrist, Hans Ulrich. *Do It: The Compendium.* New York: Independent Curators International : D.A.P./Distributed Art Publishers, 2013.

This compendium is an exhaustive gathering of instruction-based experimentation across media, sourced from the iterative, ongoing titular exhibition, Do It, curated by Hans Ulrich Obrist, who turns to editor here, bringing together instructions from over 200 artists. As sort of a meta-practicum, the curation of the show has also been approached experimentally across its iterations, and the volume includes essays contextualizing this process. Useful for creators of any stripe!

Oliveros, Pauline. *On Sonic Meditation.* La Jolla, Ca.: Center for Music

Experiment and Related Research, University of California at San Diego, 1973.

> Oliveros led a regular all-female meditation group structured by non-verbal sonic scores. Thanks to Liz Kinnamon, who reads Oliveros in relation to feminist consciousness-raising, for the tip.

Ono, Yōko. *Grapefruit: A Book of Instructions*. London: Owen, 1970.

> Ono's book of instructions, or performance scores, is also an early work of conceptual art. Selected Ono instructions can also be found online: http://www.a-i-u.net/instructions.html.

Orr, Deborah, ed. *Belief, Bodies, and Being: Feminist Reflections on Embodiment*. Lanham, Md: Rowman & Littlefield Publishers, Inc, 2006.

Puar, Jasbir K. *The Right to Maim: Debility, Capacity, Disability*. Anima. Durham: Duke University Press, 2017.

Rainer, Yvonne. *Feelings are Facts: A Life*. MIT Press, 2013.

_____, with Douglas Crimp, Maureen N McLane, and Trisha Brown. *Moving and Being Moved*, 2017.

> Both Rainer's memoir and this second collection of texts and images are a productive entry for not only movement-oriented practitioners but anyone to familiarize themselves with the changes in dance and choreography in relationship to the human body, the female body, space, and the quotidian, via choreographer-thinkers like Rainer and Brown in the 1960's through the present. Grappling with changing the field in thinking through the body and its political, disciplinary, physical and formal limitations alongside Rainer both personally and professionally is illuminating for any creative practice.

Riley, Shannon Rose, and Lynette Hunter. *Mapping Landscapes for Performance as Research: Scholarly Acts and Creative Cartographies*. New York: Palgrave Macmillan, 2009.

Russo, Linda V, and Marthe Reed. *Counter-Desecration: A Glossary for Writing within the Anthropocene*, 2018.

> A radical ecological reconfiguring and experiment in speculative etymological creative practice, Counter-Desecration gathers artists and poets to re-frame, re-define, and re-consider terminologies for the way we language our selves, our spaces, and the concepts and things and others in our field.

Schulman, Sarah. *Conflict Is Not Abuse: Overstating Harm, Community Responsibility, and the Duty of Repair*. Vancouver: Arsenal Pulp Press, 2016.

A challenging and necessary close look at the ways in which our communications lose precision as they fall into performative cultural and social categories of interacting (see: Victor Turner, Erving Goffman).

Sedgwick, Eve Kosofsky. "Paranoid Reading and Reparative Reading, or, You're So Paranoid, You Probably Think This Essay Is About You." In *Touching Feeling*, by Eve Kosofsky Sedgwick, 123–51. edited by Michèle Aina Barale, Jonathan Goldberg, and Michael Moon. Duke University Press, 2002. https://doi.org/10.1215/9780822384786-005.

Paranoid theory, in Sedgwick's formulation, is theory based on suspicion, where demystification and exposure are the core actions. The worst thing that can happen to a paranoid critic is surprise, so paranoid theory is constantly anticipating, constantly proceeding as if one can never be paranoid enough. Paranoia, when considered reductively, operates on the "cruel and contemptuous assumption that the one thing lacking for global revolution, exposure of gender roles, or whatever, is people's (that is, other people's) having the painful effects of their oppression, poverty, or deludedness sufficiently exacerbated to make the pain conscious. (as if otherwise it wouldn't have been) and intolerable (as if intolerable situations were famous for generating excellent solutions)." While most paranoid theory operates with much more nuance than this assumption, its overwhelming influence as a form of knowing means contemporary theory proceeds as if it is indeed the underlying structure. This effectively erases the non-paranoid elements in theory and epistemological approaches that are other than paranoid, impoverishing critical thought by limiting the gene pool. Exposing and naming power structures plays a central role in any movement that seeks to change the balance of power structure. But I find Sedgwick's points (1) that anxiety is deeply linked to paranoia, so that a paranoid approach will continue to produce and strengthen anxiety, and (2) that paranoid knowing assumes an endless supply of naive audience for that which it exposes, to be the most crucial arguments against relying on paranoid knowing specifically as a way of theorizing anxiety.

Sharman, Zena. *The Remedy: Queer and Trans Voices on Health and Health Care,* 2017.

Singer, Michael A, and Institute of Noetic Sciences. *The Untethered Soul: The Journey beyond Yourself,* 2013.

Sliwinski, Adam, Lynne DeSilva-Johnson (Elæ Moss), and Ain Gordon. *A Gun Show: Sō Percussion and Emily Johnson in Performance,* 2016.

Spolin, Viola. *Improvisation for the Theater: A Handbook of Teaching and Directing Techniques.* 3 edition. Evanston, Ill: Northwestern University Press, 1999.

Spradlin, RoseAnne. "Context Notes for 'Y.'" New York Live Arts, 2018.

Taylor, Diana. *The Archive and the Repertoire: Performing Cultural Memory in the Americas.* Durham: Duke University Press, 2007.
> By now canonical in performance studies but also routinely cited across disciplines, Taylor's book addresses the gap between archive (knowledge recorded in writing) and repertoire (knowledge encoded in embodied practices). A key text for theorizing how we know through our bodies.

Turner, Victor. "Social Dramas and Stories About Them," Critical Inquiry 7(1), 1980.
> Turner's framework, which he terms "social drama," breaks down iterative cultural cycles of upheaval and subsequent settling into the phases of "breach," "crisis," "redress," and "schism," a lens through which to evaluate one's own unwitting, complicit engagement in meta-cycles of human behavior.

Uzendoski, Michael A. and Edith Felicia Calapucha-Tapuy. *The Ecology of the Spoken Word: Amazonian Storytelling and Shamanism among the Napo Runa.* University of Illinois Press, 2012. https://www.jstor.org/stable/10.5406/j.ctt1xcgkj.

Van der Kolk, Bessel A. *The Body Keeps the Score: Brain, Mind, and Body in the Healing of Trauma.* New York: Viking, 2014.

Van der Kolk, Bessel A., Alexander C. McFarlane, and Lars Weisæth, eds. Traumatic Stress: *The Effects of Overwhelming Experience on Mind, Body, and Society.* New York: Guilford Press, 1996.

Van Horn, Gavin, and John Hausdoerffer, eds. Wildness: *Relations of People & Place.* Chicago: The University of Chicago Press, 2017.

Whitehouse, Mary Starks, Janet Adler, Joan Chodorow, and Patrizia Pallaro. *Authentic Movement.* London: Philadelphia : J. Kingsley Publishers, 1999.

LINKS AND ALLIES

Network of Ensemble Theaters
https://www.ensembletheaters.net/

Open Waters
http://www.open-waters.org

Eliot Feenstra
https://www.eliotfeenstra.com/

The School of Making Thinking
http://www.theschoolofmakingthinking.com/

iLAND: Interdisciplinary Laboratory for Art Nature and Dance
http://www.ilandart.org

Culture Push
http://culturepush.org

The Office of Recuperative Strategies
http://oors.net

STORMY BUDWIG I have recently focused on creating choreography that functions as a fantastical, practical, site-responsive survival strategy—while unfolding in a group sojourning, multi-hour long structure. I rehearse and experiment with turn-taking, visible choice-making, counterpoint, slow accretion, stillness, and somatics-based movement that feels familiar yet strange. These forms occur through the lens of a central proposal that the performance = an exemplary, creative (re)presentation of survival. Over the past two years I have expanded my dance-making practice to incorporate teaching and working inside of decentralized collectives. Branching out in this way encourages me to contextualize movement and physical practices in a variety of situations. This feels important to my reasons for doing ephemeral, live, iterative work in the first place. Teaching and co-facilitating, as I do here in these Precarity Bodyhacking Workshops with Cory and Elæ, is choreographic in its own way. Precarity manifests in the body, but so do other processes and strategies if we invite them in. I am eager to initiate and spread these kinds of invitations. Email me at dance@artistlivingandworking.lol to find out about upcoming processes.

BIO: stormy budwig is a dance artist living and working in Montpellier, France and nomadically across the US. stormy has presented dance projects and performance installations at the Centre Chorégraphique National Montpellier, CDCN Toulouse - La Place de la Danse, and in New York at La MaMa Moves! Festival, Center for Performance Research, McCarren Park, AUNTS, Roulette, and more. Stormy was in the *master exerce* cohort from 2019-2021 and is an active founding member of the Hungry Mothers collective researching and reconstituting an embodied commitment to the planet. She is a student of water changing form, hydropoetic expressions, and the mycelial underground that never ceases to salvage, connect, and repair. Visit https://stormchoreo.graphics to see what's brewing in the realm of dancing, facilitation, writing, and gathering.

ELÆ MOSS: For as long as I can remember, I have been driven by a fascination with evolution, and in particular, our unique capacity as an intelligent organism to constantly respond to our environment and agentively adapt and level up both our individual bodies and our collective systems and infrastructures. Inspired by biological systems -

and committed to considering our impact, always, on our environment -- my passion is helping others to learn (and build!) agile, sustainable, efficient practices and models for the best possible life lived here, together, in the anthropocene (such as it is), and to encourage Open Source / P2P sharing of our learning along the way, for the good of the whole. As a creative practitioner and a publisher, I am driven by a concern with the future of the archive as well as the ontological repercussions of that future. I strive to make, publish, and archive radical, experimental, critical work and process material that represents the most original (never the most popular) thinking happening today, most in danger of being lost to the record in an age of capital media control and a move to digitalization. I consider my interdisiciplinary practice -- and creative practice in general -- not in relationship to specific media or consumable "fields," but rather as a central channel of our species' attempt to understand itself and its environment, to mediate and communicate that both to our contemporaries and those that may follow. Whether in visual art, sound, text, dance, or so on, I see this practice as, truly, re-presentation: a sensory re-programming via a unique, original presentation of perception, experience, or cognition in material or performance form, so that both practitioner and audience may have an opportunity to experience their body / field / senses anew, and continue on in their work / life having taken on the additional data (or having been partially re-wired) via this adaptive exposure. To all these practices I bring many years of scholarship in and around the interrelationship of space, place, architecture, language, identity, perception, ideology, creative practice and the body, as well as a long personal history, training, and workshop facilitation in non-western medical traditions and healing methodologies, homeopathy, somatic practices, and mindfulness, a personal journey taken in response to coping with many years of chronic illness and precarity in my own life.

BIO: Elæ Moss (b. Lynne DeSilva-Johnson, 1979) is a nonbinary neuroqueer disabled multimodal creator and performer, cultural scholar, and educator. Their work of building Speculative Solidarities employs experimentation across analog and digital media to consider intersections between persons, forms of language, and systems, directed towards seeding resilient, open source strategies for ecological and social change. Elæ is the founder and creative director of The Operating System & Liminal Lab, a radical open source arts organization, online platform, peer learning and publishing initiative. Prior to coming to Pratt, they taught in the CUNY system for 10 years, in addition to serving as a teaching artist for myriad organizations and schools for learners of all ages, and working for many years in the trenches of NYC's hospitality and service industries. They are dedicated to the development of and access to collective learning models, tools, and resources, and in 2019 founded Liminal Lab, an open access peer learning platform, as an extension of the OS. [see https://www.theoperatingsystem.org/liminal-lab/] Elæ's work and performances have appeared widely. Recently, they presented [MOVE SEMANTICS]: RULES of UNFOLDING, co-curated with Jeff Kasper as part of EFA Project Space's "BRIGHT FUTURES" awarded season.

Other recent projects include: the APRIORI Field Station at STWST/Ars Electronica, R&D with the Mycelium Network Society, the Speculative Resilience Radical Practice Library for Bushwick Open Studios and the Anarchist Bookfair at Judson Church, How to Human: Disruptor Mechanism Protocol for the Segal Center's Performing Knowledge Festival, Building Interpersonal Infrastructures at SOHO20, and Collaborative Precarity Bodyhacking with stormy budwig and Cory Tamler for the Exponential Festival. Publication credits include Vestiges, Big Echo: Critical SF, Tagvverk, Matters of Feminist Practice, The Transgender Narratives Anthology, Choice Words: Writers on Abortion, the Urgent Possibilities: Feminist Poetics & Pedagogies annex series, and many more. Books include Ground, Blood Altas, Overview Effect, Sweet and Low: Indefinite Singular, Bodies of Work (in collaboration with painter Georgia Elrod), and The Precarity Bodyhacking Work-Book and Guide. Find and follow their social practice projects online via IG @thetroublewithbartleby, or at http://onlywhatican.net.

CORY TAMLER: I come to this work via my ongoing interest in performance-as-research, community-based theatre work, pedagogy, and cross-disciplinary research and thinking. In my early training in writing and theatre I was taught to approach creative work as an individual artist first—collaboration was an afterthought, if it came at all. Horizontal artistic practices were something I had to discover on my own. My first professional gig as a playwright was as part of a community-based theatre project with Open Waters (Portland, ME, 2010-11), influenced by the work of LA-based company Cornerstone. This process taught me two things that have guided my practice ever since. The first is that working to create something good together (by which I mean something of which everyone involved is proud, whether that's a performance, piece of art or writing, event, or something else) is the best way of building community and having difficult conversations that span ideologies, backgrounds, identities.

The second is that when you learn something new through the body, it adds an entirely different dimension of understanding. My work since then has used performance practices learned from ensemble companies, community-based theatremakers, the work of community organizers and activists, and my peers to build containers for making thinking together in ways that disrespect the Cartesian mind/body dichotomy and the Wagnerian stage/auditorium divide. I do not intend for this work to fall in line with the experience economy; I don't believe that an artwork can make possible some kind of human interaction that is inherently elevated above interactions we can have on the street, in the baths, on the subway, at the bodega, at a protest, in the grocery store, at work. And one of the worst things you can do, unless you're Tierra Whack, is make an artwork for its Instagrammability. But I believe that doing the work has transformative power: we learn what it means to work within an arbitrary aesthetic/temporal frame, we learn how to compromise and how to speak the language (often nonverbal) of the thing we're making, we discover that there are kinds of truth that aren't about facts, we fight for something without knowing why, we learn to stand behind our choices and simultaneously that those choices can fail. This learning belongs to the making, not the experiencing, of an artwork, and it's why I often work with non-artists, and in ways that invite an exchange of knowledge and tactics. It's in this spirit of cross-disciplinary horizontal learning that I'm approaching precarity, and from a specific recent experience, too, of hosting precarity consciousness-raising circles in Brooklyn (with Amanda Friedman, following a model developed by Eliot Feenstra in Toronto). Working with stormy and Elæ to create an embodied encounter with precarity has felt like a vital counterpart to these discursive CR circles. If you would like to join our Brooklyn circles, which meet monthly in the spirit of an ongoing study group, please write: corytamler@gmail.com.

BIO: Cory Tamler is a writer, translator, and interdisciplinary artist whose practice is rooted in theatre, performance as research, and community organizing. She currently co-facilitates/creates work with the Penobscot River watershed and In Kinship Fellowship as a core artist with Open Waters in Wabanaki/Maine. A former Fulbright scholar, she has created and participated in research-based performance projects in the United States, Germany, and Serbia, and has worked with museums and companies including the New Museum for Contemporary Art, The Civilians, the Martin E. Segal Theatre Center, the James Gallery, Sprat Artistic Ensemble, Yinzerspielen, and the School of Making Thinking. She is a member of the editorial team of the GrayLit Culture Hub and a Ph.D. candidate in the Program in Theatre and Performance at The Graduate Center, CUNY, where she also co-coordinates the Social Practice CUNY initiative. Her dissertation research, which has been supported with awards from the DAAD (German Academic Exchange Service) and Art & Science Connect, compares contemporary experimental practice in physics and performance.Yinzerspielen, and the School of Making Thinking. A core artist with civic arts organization Open Waters (Maine), Cory has written a play about small-scale farming and a book of performance scores based on migratory fish. Cory was a Fulbright Scholar (Berlin) and her academic and critical writing and translations have been published in The Mercurian, Studies in Musical Theatre, Asymptote, Culturebot, The Offing, Extended Play, Howlround, and SCENA. As a Ph.D. student in Theatre and Performance at The Graduate Center, CUNY, she studies open-ended artistic work from social practice to community-based theatre.

PROJECT DESIGN / / EXTENDED COLOPHON:

The original limited edition printing of this Work-Book and Guide was released in January 2019, timed to coincide with and be used by participants in our Collaborative Precarity Bodyhacking workshop as part of stormy's then residency, *Resistance Fantasies,* at the Target Margin theater in Brooklyn, New York. We produced more of them, as explained earlier, so that this resource and guide could be used for independent and/or collective / community study, indeed also providing the tools for running a similar workshop to ours.

The book was designed by me (Elæ Moss) with feedback from Cory and stormy as we gathered and developed the resources and exercises herein. It was designed to be understated, feeling more like a tool or notebook to use than the work of someone else -- while it does operate as "Social Practice," its goals are genuine / use, not art or the performance of care, as such. If you were holding a book from the original printing in your hand it might feel like an old school grammar school workbook, or remind you of early to mid 20th century experimental practice, with the interior pages printed over a light background grid, reinforcing the "technical" aesthetic. It's sized intentionally at 5.5" x 8.5" so that it could, if desired, be reproduced from its PDF form for community use on a standard printer. For the cover stock of that edition I chose a natural, heavier craft-paper with some fiber apparent, and the cover itself only had the title in all caps in a thin rectangular box near the top of the page, with our names below, both in small type.

The typeface throughout is Freight Sans, a modern typeface designed by Black American type designer Joshua Darden. Many typefaces are part of an ethically compromised history, and through my work with the OS/LL project, amplifying modern designers (especially BIPOC who are so often invisible in the craft) is central.
More at https://www.dardenstudio.com

This second edition, produced in 2021 so that the work could be accessed by a global audience using the distribution networks of the OS's publications, retains the interior elements of the first while playing on the initial cover design in digital replica, with a description on the back, which previously did not appear.

- Elæ Moss, Brooklyn NY / Lenapehoking, 2021

DOC U MENT
/däkyəmənt/

First meant "instruction" or "evidence," whether written or not.

noun - a piece of written, printed, or electronic matter that provides
information or evidence or that serves as an official record
verb - record (something) in written, photographic, or other form
synonyms - paper - deed - record - writing - act - instrument

[*Middle English, precept, from Old French, from Latin
documentum, example, proof, from docre, to teach; see dek- in
Indo-European roots.*]

Who is responsible for the manufacture of value?

Based on what supercilious ontology have we landed in a space
where we vie against other creative people in vain pursuit
of the fleeting credibilities of the scarcity economy, rather than
freely collaborating and sharing openly with each other
in ecstatic celebration of MAKING?

While we understand and acknowledge the economic pressures and fear-mongering
that threatens to dominate and crush the creative impulse, we also believe that
now more than ever we have the tools to relinquish agency via cooperative means,
fueled by the fires of the Open Source Movement.

**Looking out across the invisible vistas of that rhizomatic parallel country
we can begin to see our community beyond constraints,
in the place where intention meets
resilient, proactive, collaborative organization.**

Here is a document born of that belief, sown purely of imagination and will.
When we document we assert. We print to make real, to reify our being there.
When we do so with mindful intention to address our process, to open our work
to others, to create beauty in words in space, to respect and acknowledge
the strength of the page we now hold physical, a thing in our hand,
we remind ourselves that, like Dorothy:
we had the power all along, my dears.

THE PRINT! DOCUMENT SERIES
is a project of
the trouble with bartleby
in collaboration with
the operating system